WATERCOLOURS

BY

ALBRECHT DÜRER

—

THIRTY-TWO PLATES IN COLOUR

SELECTED AND WITH AN INTRODUCTION

BY ANNA MARIA CETTO

—

THE MACMILLAN COMPANY · NEW YORK

HOLBEIN-VERLAG · BASEL

First published in the English language in 1954
Translated from the German language by Glyn T. Hughes

Printed in the Netherlands

ALBRECHT DÜRER
1471–1528

As the son of a worthy goldsmith in Nuremberg the young Dürer started in his father's workshop. Then he was apprenticed to the painter Michael Wolgemut from 1484 to 1490. His father did not make a goldsmith of him, and his world renown is not based on his paintings, yet he owes to these two teachers the foundation for what has brought him immortality—his graphic art.

He had become familiar in his father's workshop with engraving in copper, for it was the goldsmiths who knew how to work figures on plates with a burin, and who had just discovered, a few decades before, that prints could be pulled from them. Woodcutting Dürer learned from Wolgemut, in whose workshop were prepared along the years the pictorial blocks for the most important Nuremberg books of the time, for the *Schatzbehalter* (*The Treasury*) and for Hartmann Schedel's *Weltchronik* (*World-Chronicle*), which were to be printed by Dürer's godfather Anton Koberger.

Dürer later brought the woodcut and the engraving to a pitch of perfection never achieved by anyone after him. With them he made his appearance as artist, printer and editor, independent of outside orders. These small-format works, within reach of hundreds who could never in all their life have dreamt of commissioning a painting, made Dürer great. He could choose their subjects himself and allow his remarkable inventive spirit to flow unchecked through them. They were known to everyone, and, disseminated north and south, spread his fame at the same time as his compositions. For Dürer the engraver and woodcutter was already held in high esteem by his contemporaries, even by his critical Venetian colleagues and the exacting masters of the Netherlands. Even Raphael paid homage to him by sending him one of his drawings.

Moreover Dürer was a great master of drawing and a most excellent watercolourist. This, though, was known only to a very few, to his best friends, such as the scholarly Willibald Pirkheimer (see pp. 21, 25 f.), and individual patrons, such as the Emperor Maximilian I, who had his prayer-book embellished with exquisite pen drawings. The coloured brush drawings and the watercolour paintings, however, were mostly destined for the artist's own portfolio of studies (Plates 2–17, 19–21, 23–25, 30–31), only in very rare instances for a patron (Plate 22); occasionally too for another artist as a model-drawing for a work in gold, for a chandelier (Plate 26), or for a costume (Plate 28).

Thus Dürer's contemporaries scarcely knew what a gifted artist he was when he was not spending months employing costly oils on carefully prepared panels, but just painting studies and sketches which he executed with the least expensive material of all, watercolours on paper. And still less did they guess what a pioneering and really original landscape artist was at work here, attempting things which were not to occur to painters again for several centuries, painting in watercolours as a *pleinairiste* a brief impression of sunrise or evening glow or a landscape damp after thunder (Plates 11–13). The Venetian artists, with whose warm coloration Dürer's oil paintings can certainly not compete, may well, however, have secretly recognized that the brilliancy of his brush studies on their natural blue paper surpassed everything they themselves had hitherto achieved in this technique (Plates 19–21). In the Netherlands, too, it will have become clear during his visit that there was nobody to compete with him in his brush portraits and still-life work (Plates 30, 31).

These beautiful coloured sheets present us with many problems. How did Dürer start using the watercolour, and what subjects did he choose for preference? What technical processes did he employ? For his sheets differ not only one from another, but, even more, from the watercolours of modern artists; thus his famous *Hare* (Plate 16) looks quite different from, for example, the rapidly applied wash of a Cézanne watercolour. Then, too, there is the question of whether in these works there is mirrored something of the gradual maturing of the man Dürer and of his style, something of his conception of life and art.

We shall try to find some slight clue to such matters as we trace the course of the artist's life, and see how the works reproduced in this book are woven into it.

Having outgrown Michael Wolgemut's workshop Dürer began at Easter 1490 a four-year journey 'through Germany.' Where he went altogether between 1490 and 1492 before he came to Colmar, Basle and Strasbourg, we cannot say with certainty, but it is probable that he worked in the region of Mainz and Frankfurt, in Cologne and in the Netherlands. His drawings testify to the attraction for him of the 'Housebook Master,' a very lively, humorous illustrator who was certainly active in the Central Rhineland. Dürer knew what he wanted, and here there was much for him to learn in the way of keen observation of real life, of assured presentation in graphic terms, of confident choice of unconventional subject matter.

The *Young Couple* (Plate 1) riding to the chase, the main motif of whose figures is directly suggested by this master, remains wholly Dürer's own in its pictorial composition. He is following ideas common to his generation when, with the Housebook Master, with his friend Pirkheimer and many others, he believes the nature and destiny of the individual to be influenced by the disposition of the stars at the hour of his birth. Despite all the late Gothic arabesque of the form, the way in which he characterizes the generous, enterprising and happy nature of the 'Children of Jupiter' by the composition, by the spirited and joyful qualities of man and beast, by eryngo, the plant of good fortune, is almost childlike in its directness and simplicity, if one contrasts the way in which, about twenty years later, he achieved a powerful reading of the melancholic temperament in his profound and richly symbolic engraving *Melencolia*. The sheet with the 'Young Couple' is so pictorially finished that one may well suppose it to have been specially produced, perhaps for the wedding of a friend: the Basle costume (also found

4

in woodcuts which Dürer made for Basle publishers in 1492/93) suggests that the recipient of this delightful gift was a native of Basle.

From the point of view of workmanship the picture is a pen drawing with a watercolour wash. This composite technique, which Dürer favoured for the watercolour painting of his compositions in picture form (Plates 18, 32) had hitherto been chiefly used in the illustration of books written on paper. Later Dürer also completed in the same way the final sketch for the pictures he planned, and gave it to the customer as a project drawing when the commission was granted (Plate 22). The process was particularly well adapted for this purpose, because it fixed the composition unmistakably and at the same time indicated the prevailing colour atmosphere only to an extent which still allowed free play to the artist in the finishing of details during his protracted work at the panel. Even if he himself only sketched out the work for others to execute— for a frame-carver (Plate 22) or a court tailor (Plate 28)—this kind of drawing with watercolour painting, in which contours and modelling were clearly traced in with the pen, was an excellent means of imparting information.

Shortly after his return to Nuremberg and newly married, he set out for Venice in the autumn of 1494 in order to escape the plague in his native town, and to meet Pirkheimer who was studying in Pavia—this at least is the usual explanation, as if it were enough to explain why the choice should then fall on Venice. He went there, we may be sure, with the certainty that a new world would open for him as an artist, for he was already acquainted with compositions by Andrea Mantegna who was active in neighbouring Padua and Mantua, and who in addition was related by marriage to Giovanni Bellini whom Dürer held in especial honour in Venice. Perhaps, too, he had already heard about it earlier in Mainz from that original painter Erhard Reuwich, who in 1486 had embellished Breidenbach's *Reise ins Heilige Land* (*Journey to the Holy Land*) with his woodcuts of towns, of Jerusalem and Venice, of strange beasts and costumes. For these are the subjects which now particularly attract Dürer's attention on his travels.

How greatly he marvelled at the warlike sea-animal he came across in Venice is shown just by the size of the study he devoted to a Mediterranean crab (Plate 2). And now the painter in him awakes, and the most important thing for him is not to fix the forms in linear work but to reproduce the coloured appearance in watercolour painting, after first lightly sketching the main outlines on the paper with a stylus. In doing this he worked differently from modern painters who apply their colour in quite wet and transparent washes and who leave the white-grounded paper for the highest lights. Bright patches are often put on as heightening by Dürer using white body colour. Altogether in his watercolour paintings he most frequently uses the watercolour in conjunction with body colour (Plates 2, 3, 5, 6, 9–14, 16, 17, 25), particularly when, with the finest brush, he is putting in detail such as the delicate hairs in the coat of the *Hare* (Plate 16). Often he works with such a pointed squeezed-out brush that he can put in

5

the contours as sharply as with a pen, and one hesitates as to whether they are not indeed drawn with a pen (Plate 3).

It is as if the sight of the watery shimmer of the city of lagoons and the wealth of good pictures by Carpaccio and Cima, by the Bellinis and Mantegna, had not only opened the young Dürer's eyes, but had also inspired him with a manly self-confidence. For on the journey home from Venice, Dürer, stimulated by the wonderful landscape backgrounds which Giovanni Bellini had created out of his imagination for his figure pictures, dares to record actual landscapes and towns as seen in nature (Plates 3–7). His incredibly sharp eye submits itself to a self-imposed task which is wholly new as an undertaking, and in the attainment of an almost scientific topographical actuality. Moreover, as works of art these landscapes are quite incomparable. For the first time his genius breaks through quite freely with something new and peculiar to itself. Yet how inseparably and impenetrably that which was only to be observed faithfully and precisely in nature is fused with that which he draws from the 'secret treasury of the heart' (to use his own words)!

There will have been no little amazement at Nuremberg in the Wolgemut workshop at such prospects of towns as those of Arco, Trento and Innsbruck (Plates 3, 5, 7). The pictures of towns in the *World-Chronicle* of Hartmann Schedel could not compare, proud though they could be of them. Despite the fact that these woodcuts had come out only two years earlier they must, with their late Gothic bird's-eye perspective, have appeared old and outmoded. In their insipidness and at the same time their topographical inexactness they are the direct opposite of Dürer's watercolours, in which, in addition, we find sunshine and the play of water, and feel the breath and breadth of the natural world (Plate 6).

Dürer's landscapes gave rise to no school in their time; they were too far ahead of it.

Having dared and achieved such things, and being now domiciled in Nuremberg as an independent artist, Dürer could well trust himself to turn to the prodigious work, *Apocalypse*. It is from this time between 1495 and 1500, when, in youthful consciousness of his own powers and 'inwardly full of figures,' as he himself expresses it, he displayed the greatest delight in creating, that our plates 8–14 derive.

Besides executing commissions for pictures, and more than sixty engravings and woodcuts, which he himself cut and printed on his own press, he found time for making studies from nature in the open air. In a quarry he completed a whole series of sheets in different techniques, our example being remarkable for the verve of its execution (Plate 8). Here for once (and it is a very rare occurrence for him) the strokes are made with a brush trimmed broad and are applied transparent wash by wash, whilst for the *Fir-Tree* (Plate 10) he again made use of body colour.

At the time when, in the *Apocalypse* sheets, in the black and white of the woodcut, he makes fire and stars fall from heaven, storms rage and the earth spew out sheaves of water, he is painting in watercolours the most fabulous miracles of colour. For the city of *Nuremberg* (Plate 9) he has chosen an almost startling view and unforgettable tones:

6

green and brownish violet give the foreground the heaviness of earth, while the farthest houses float in the delicate light blue of the atmosphere and of the radiance of the sun.

In storm and stress he frees himself from the cool bluish-green which is predominant in the landscapes of the Italian journey (Plates 3, 5, 6), and seeks those moments when the world is lying bathed in most colour (Plates 11–13). It is no longer the range of valleys and hills (Plate 6), the crystalline forms of rocks and houses (Plates 3, 4) which captivate him. It is the emotional appeal of the play of colour which transports him. In every sheet a colour peals out like the note of an organ: reddish-yellow in the *House on an Island in a Pond* (Plate 11), blue in the *Pond in the Woods* (Plate 12), emerald green in the unique *Mills on a River* (Plate 13). Only two other landscapes, those of *Kalchreuth* (Plate 25), follow, and this probably more than ten years later. The earlier glow of colour has yielded to the light of late summer, whose warmer beams move us just as deeply as the artist's great maturity.

Simultaneously with assiduous work at his engravings Dürer about the turn of the century learned how to draw with great certainty just using a pressed-out watercolour brush. This is shown by the three masterly studies of a *Jousting Helmet* (Plate 14). The first was begun with a preparatory pen drawing, quickly abandoned in order to proceed using the brush alone, with which, we may notice especially, he hatches the gorget of the second dry in cross-coats, and gives a dark border to the cords and straps, while he paints other parts in a wash. The costume study of the *Nuremberg Lady Dressed for Church* (Plate 15) was first drawn wholly with the brush and then washed lightly with delicate colours, as he later did for the *Little Chandelier Woman* (Plate 26) and *Arion* (Plate 27), both of which he finishes off by strengthening the outlines with the point of the pen.

In the *Jousting Helmet* and the *Nuremberg Lady* we see over Dürer's shoulder how he trains his imagination, for it was to such studies as much as anything that he owed his unusual memory for forms. With patient devotion he dedicates the same penetrating urgency to creatures of the natural world, to the *Hare* (Plate 16) and to the *Great Piece of Turf* (Plate 17). The miracle achieved by Dürer in this direction may be grasped by anyone who will go to the trouble of opening an edition of *Hortus Sanitatis*, the most important animal and plant picture-book of the time. Two signs in the *Hare* of 1502 show Dürer speaking his own language: the monogram, found here for the first time in this magnificent and final form, attests with special pride—This is the work of Albrecht Dürer; and with the mirroring in the eye of the cross-bars of the window (which cannot be shown in reproductions) he adds—It is in his workshop that he has made this living counterfeit of the hare.

Within this time of devoted concern with beast and plant there falls, too, the serene work at the *Life of the Virgin*, which Dürer was illustrating in a series of woodcuts. His inner occupation with such matters led his poetic genius to blossom into fairest flower in the sheet: *Madonna with a Multitude of Animals* (Plate 18). Dürer places the Madonna like a new Eve in an earthly paradise in which flowers and beasts press around her,

—clearly an original idea of his own which could not find expression in the *Life of the Virgin* because this was associated with scenes from the Bible and familiar legends.

In 1505 the plague again broke out in Nuremberg. Once more Dürer fled from it, first to Augsburg, in order to continue his journey to Venice, possibly in the hope that he would be entrusted with the paintings for the new Fondaco dei Tedeschi, a building belonging to the Venetian Government which the German merchants only rented. But he had to be content with a few commissions for panel pictures.

As preparatory work for the painting of the *Feast of the Rose Garlands* he made studies in brush drawing on natural blue paper, which had been produced recently, and solely, in Venice (Plates 19, 20). He probably took over the technique from Carpaccio, who, however, worked almost exclusively with vertical strokes, which crowd rather close together on the paper. Dürer wielded the brush with much greater freedom. Within the figure the blue corresponds to the local colour of flesh and dress on which he superimposes in black, form-shaping, parallel and cross layers the modelling in shadow, and in white that in light. There is always a triad of Blue-Black-White, and thus an essentially different play of values from the Black-White of the engraving and the woodcut, where the light ground must at the same time produce the highest degree of brightness. A powerfully plastic and thrillingly lifelike portrait is that of an *Architect* (Plate 19), which constitutes one of those studies from nature for the *Feast of the Rose Garlands* that Dürer drew directly from the model. On the other hand he created the ideal picture which he held of the beauty of a music-making messenger of heaven in the curly head of an *Angel* (Plate 20), lifting up his fervent eyes and opening his lips to sing.

Inspired by the Italians and particularly by Leonardo's artistic doctrines, Dürer interested himself most assiduously in theoretical investigations. In the spirit of the Renaissance, the 'regrowth' (*Wiedererwachsung*) as he so well calls it, he explores the laws of beauty, particularly in the human body, the secret lying for him in the best proportions: "Proper proportion gives good form." As he praises the Italians greatly for their "naked pictures," it is not surprising that his most beautiful brush drawing of a nude follows Giorgione (Plate 21). The absence of circles, dividing lines and indications of measurements, in contrast to most sheets of nudes from the Venetian time, does not mean that this must be a pure study from nature. It is just that, as in a completed work of art, they do not appear; which does not at all mean to say that this harmonious figure is not based on an ordered proportioning.

With the fear that at home he would "shiver for the sun" Dürer returned to Nuremberg in January 1507. Important commissions for paintings there awaited the successful artist. The pen and watercolour drawing for the *All Saints Picture* (Plate 22) in the Old Men's Home, a sketch which includes both the pictorial composition and the frame, is a delightful example of a project drawing to accompany a contract, such as Dürer used to hand to the patron on receipt of a commission.

A similar sheet will also have been handed to Jakob Heller, juror and town-councillor

8

in Frankfurt on Main, but it has not survived. We possess, however, splendid individual studies for an altar-piece commissioned by him (Plates 23, 24). At first sight they resemble the Venetian brush drawings, except that this time the paper chosen is not coloured but white, and it is carefully covered with blue (Plate 24), usually with green over pink (Plate 23), forming a sensitive painting ground which allows of no correction during the work, and which thus demands the highest certainty. In sheets like the *Standing Apostle* and the unforgettable *Hands Joined in Prayer* Dürer realized what he had promised Heller in a letter: if God will only once more give him the power he will paint "what not many people could do." Dürer, that is to say, saw artistic creation as an inspiration by grace from above, insofar as something really original was conceived and the highest quality attained; and this is just what is achieved only by a chosen few of the many who are called.

With the study of the Hands Dürer proves himself a master of inspired detail. The greatly conceived, unified composition *Kalchreuth* (Plate 25) testifies in the realm of landscape to his maturity as a pictorial modeller, as does the *All Saints Sketch* (Plate 22) in the realm of the altar-panel. Merely in the choice of the high viewpoint and of the centralized composition Dürer has worked formal equivalents for the universal thought of the communion of all saints or of the Civitas Dei into the very basis of the picture's construction, to say nothing of the profound exposition of the basic idea of the picture in the various groups and individual figures. The following years were devoted to the graphic media and painting receded into the background. The masterly engravings of 1513–14, the *Knight, Death and Devil* and the *Melencolia* were prepared for by Dürer merely with pen studies. At the same time the work for the Emperor Maximilian I was going on, the extensive emblematic woodcut work for the *Triumphal Arch* and the *Triumphal Chariot*. The most beautiful watercolours of this period (Plates 26–28) give an effect of slight self-indulgence after the brooding above the *Melencolia*, like a cheerful play of the brush to recover from the humanistic burden of ideas in the imperial woodcuts. The *Little Chandelier Woman*, a sketch of a lamp for Pirkheimer, is roguish and full of humour, like Dürer's letters to him; *Arion*, gaily drawn with a brush, is washed as lightly with thin colour as the tale of the singer rescued by a dolphin is buoyantly told! Luxurious fashion and a variegated play of colour characterize a *Courtly Garb* (Plate 28) which Dürer devised for a splendid show at the imperial court.

Once more Dürer undertook a long journey. In the middle of 1520 he and his wife and the maid set out for the Netherlands, probably with the primary intention of having confirmed by the new Emperor, Charles V, the annual allowance made to him by Maximilian. An equally important reason, though, as it seems to me, was to look at the town-hall pictures in Cologne and the rich cities of Holland, Flanders and Brabant, for it was only a month after his return in 1521 that he delivered to the Nuremberg Town-Council the sketches for the fresco decorations in the great chamber of the town-hall. Both religious contemplation among the followers of Luther and the encounter with the art of the Masters Wilhelm and Stephan Lochner in Cologne, with the works of the Master of Flémalle and Rogier, of Dieric Bouts and Massys, and all the others in the Netherlands, caused Dürer in his last decade to become a portraitist and figure-painter of grave sublimity.

Only three head studies were, exceptionally, painted with size colours on canvas, a technique which he only very seldom used for smaller paintings. The sketch for the *Head of a Madonna* (Plate 29) shows the late style by its austere grandeur.

With the studies for a picture of *St. Jerome* (Plates 30, 31), Dürer brought brush drawing on colour-grounded paper to highest perfection. Into the bearing and lineaments of the old man who sat as his model he has already read a saintly Jerome lost in profound meditation on death and the Scriptures. What a distance he had come from the Cardinal Jerome extracting the thorn from the lion's paw in the Basle woodcut of 1492, and from the assiduously writing and saintly translator of the Bible in the masterly engraving of 1514! The *Reading-Desk*, too, is carefully studied from nature in a sheet which breathes a wonderful repose (Plate 31).

Two years before Dürer succumbed to slow fever, which he had contracted in the Netherlands, he sent to the Nuremberg Town-Council in 1526 his *Apostle Panels*, a truly monumental legacy to his native town. From the same period comes the watercolour sheet with the *Annunciation* (Plate 32), which with its loose composition and decorative magnificence, with the freedom of movement of the figures, stands alone in the master's late work as a promise of new directions for his genius.

NOTES ON THE PLATES

I

Young Couple on Horseback

Pen and watercolour. 215 × 165 mm. At the top the date 1496. The scrawled ('*geschleuderte*')
monogram below has been inserted by another hand. Probably from the year 1496,
perhaps after a drawing from the travel years 1490–1494.
Formerly Berlin, Staatliches Kupferstichkabinett.

The sheet, a delicate pen drawing coloured with watercolours and with a line as a border framing it, strives for an integral pictorial effect. This, and notably too the spirited and joyful quality of the whole, gives it an outstanding position amongst the early figurative sheets of the young Dürer.

Tree-trunk and hound, horse and saddlecloth are in the same way found again in Dürer's woodcut with *Knight and Lansquenet* (Bartsch 131), which is supposed to date from about 1497.

The affinity of the riding couple with that in the picture of the planet Jupiter in the Middle-Ages *Housebook* of Wolfegg Castle, dating from about 1480 and also, it may be added, a pictorially constructed pen drawing, has been justly pointed out (Tietze).

The couple dressed in the Basle fashion almost have a smile on their faces as they gallop away with the hound baying around them. It seems to me that more than just the formal motif of the couple riding to the chase has been suggested by the Housebook Master. The symbolism, too, originates there: the couple riding along here are blissful children of Jupiter, and we may apply to them those lines which are found in the *Housebook*:

> Modest, virtuous and plain,
> Wise, peaceful, well-bred, just,
> Blissful, well-adorned and noble,
> Fair, genteel, intelligent,
> A pretty, rosy countenance
> As if designed for laughing.
> Horse, falcon and the lure,
> And hunting to the hounds they pursue.
> Judge, marksman and scholar,
> Lawyer, draughtsman and lover
> Are attracted to these things
> When wholly children of Jupiter.

Medieval astrology counted as an enviable child of Jupiter anyone at whose birth the planet Jupiter appeared in the sign of Pisces or Sagittarius. The eryngo, too, springing from the earth behind the horse, accords with that as the symbol of good sport and success in love.

What judge or huntsman, scholar or lawyer, one wonders, was the blissful child of Jupiter for whom Dürer drew this late Gothically decorative little sheet.

Sea Crab

Watercolours and white body colour. Preliminary sketch with a stylus. 263 × 355 mm.
Probably dating from 1495 in Venice.
Vierhouten, D. G. van Beuningen Collection.

It is not surprising that it was on his first Italian journey that Dürer began to make studies of living animals; for North Italy was highly advanced in this direction. After Giovannino de' Grassi had already at the end of the 14th century painted in his sketchbook red deer, falcons and eagles (obviously from princely parks), and Pisanello about the middle of the 15th century had achieved incomparable results with his magnificent watercolours of tame and wild animals, Leonardo was now producing there animal studies with the sharply delineating silverpoint and with the pen.

We possess of Dürer's the large format watercolour of a lobster, signed and dated 1495 (Winkler 91). It shows, as has been zoologically determined, a specimen belonging to an Adriatic species. The origin of the animal and the dating of the sheet place it therefore during the period of Dürer's first Venetian visit. Following this drawing the crab could also be recognized as Dürer's work and classified as an *Eriphia spinifrons*, which is often to be met with at rocky spots on the shores of the Adriatic. The colours show that the sheet must have been painted from a living animal.

In the bottom right-hand corner of the famous *Madonna with a Multitude of Animals* (Plate 18) there is another crab, which is, however, not drawn from our study but from memory or from some other sheet which has not survived.

Arco

Water and body colour. Details outlined finely with the pen. 221 × 221 mm. Top right Dürer's
inscription 'fenedier klawsen' and the monogram added by another hand.
Produced in 1495 on the journey back from Venice.
Paris, Musée du Louvre.

On his journey home from Venice in the spring of 1495 Dürer made his way from Verona to Trento via Arco, which dominates the Valley of Sarca north of Lake Garda.

With a sure touch the artist reinforces the effect of weight in the mountain massif by the unusual square format of the picture.

The main motif, the mountain, dominates without reservation. Away beyond the foreground's brownish soil which the artist still just keeps in view, he has directed his gaze on to the towering rocky mass, all the details of which he observes with keen-eyed affection, and he completely omits the Alpine peaks rising behind it.

Houses and towers, walls and rocks lie, clear and hard as crystal, in the light of the morning sun. The bluish tops of the olive trees and the bright green vines in the vineyard to the right are bearing their spring foliage.

The Castle of Trento

4

Watercolour. 198 × 257 mm. Top right Dürer's inscription 'trint.'
Produced in 1495 on the journey back from Venice.
London, British Museum.

This careful study of the Castello di Buon Consiglio agrees pretty exactly with the edifice itself, in so far as it has survived. Not much attention is paid to the foreground; it is given only a quick wash with the brush. But the details of the fortification, of the battlements, oriels and windows are what interest Dürer. This is not surprising since he must have undertaken a special digression from the main route of his journey in order to see the Arco stronghold (Plate 3).

Such studies are early harbingers of his Manual of Fortification which he published in 1527 under the title: *Etliche underricht zu befestigung der Stett Schloss und flecken.*

Trento seen from the North

5

Water and body colours. 238 × 356 mm. At the top Dürer's inscription 'Trȳt,'
and alongside the monogram, added by another hand.
Produced in 1495 on the journey back from Venice.
Formerly Bremen, Kunsthalle.

Dürer was not concerned with registering exactly the various details as he was in the view of the Castle (Plate 4).

In a few uncompromising colours he set out broadly the landscape in which Trento is embedded as though it had been pushed to one side by the river. In the foreground the Adige reflects the city and a blue wood which dominate the middle distance. In the rear bright sunshine lies violet on the bare Dolomites.

As the course of the Adige was during the last century moved more than a quarter of a mile to the west the view of the river is no longer to be seen from where Dürer stood.

South-Tyrolean Mountain Scene

6

Water and body colours. 210 × 312 mm. Top right Dürer's inscription 'welsch pirg'
(Welsches Gebirge—Italian Mountains).
Probably produced in 1495 on the journey back from Venice.
Oxford, Ashmolean Museum.

The sheet, like most of the landscape studies made by Dürer on the journey home, is unfinished. This is because of the way in which it arose and the problem facing Dürer; there was no suggestion of producing a finished 'picture.'

The foreground and middle distance are broadly dashed off, as is the rear mountain chain in the background, with the bright clouds of morning floating over it. It was only over the mountain in the central part of the sheet that Dürer really took pains.

The scene has been determined as in the region near Segonzano in the Val di Cembra, east of Trento.

Modern art history shows in this case a desire to be even more 'exact' than the artist himself. How instructive it is, though, that Dürer did not give the scene its proper name but just a generic title as caption. He did not want to seize what was peculiar to a particular scene, but rather the morning splendour of mountain summits rising one behind another like ocean waves.

7   *Innsbruck seen from the North*

Watercolour. 127 × 187 mm. Top right Dürer's inscription 'Isprug' and the
monogram added by another hand.
Probably produced in 1495 on the journey back from Venice.
Vienna, Albertina.

As in the *Castle of Trento* (Plate 4), the buildings of Innsbruck are precisely delineated in all their details. This sheet, however, is a finished watercolour picture, and how wonderfully finished!

The many-towered city on the Inn forms a complete whole dominated by a mountain still wearing the snows of spring. It lies, a solid region of earth, stretched between the scudding clouds and the flowing waters in which it is reflected.

The artist who had made youthful and awkward watercolours at Nuremberg of the *Cemetery of St. John's* and the *Wire-drawing Mill* (Winkler 61 and 62) would scarcely have achieved this *Innsbruck* on the journey out to Venice. The little masterpiece presupposes, as it seems to me, both the sight of the city of lagoons and of its painting and also much eager study on his own account (cf. Plates 3–6).

8   *Quarry*

Watercolour. 232 × 197 mm. Top left Dürer's inscription 'steinpruch' and
later monogram. Produced about 1495 after the return from Italy.
Milan, Biblioteca Ambrosiana.

In a quarry outside the walls of Nuremberg, probably the 'Schmausenbuck' with its red blocks of stone, Dürer studied rock formations. Which of his colleagues would have taken it into his head to do that?

As testimony to this we possess some sheets (Winkler 106–112) in pen drawing or pen and watercolour, or even in pure brush technique, like this magnificent dashed-off study in particular. This was for Dürer anything but a completed work of art, and it aims to be no more than a study from nature.

It became, too, a working drawing for the background of a composition. For Dürer used the sheet as a model for the main motif, the rock, in the *Penance of St. John Chrysostom* (about 1495, Bartsch 63), one of his earliest engravings.

What creative vigour and what a conception of form this young, still unpractised graphic artist must have possessed to succeed in translating these yellow, red and green brush washes into the sharp black lines of an engraving.

Nuremberg seen from the West

Water and body colours. 163 × 344 mm. Above, Dürer's inscription 'Nörnperg'
and the monogram added by another hand.
About 1495/1497 after the return from Italy.
Formerly Bremen, Kunsthalle.

Dürer is standing outside the ramparts in the district between the Tiergärtner Gate and the New Gate when he takes in this view, that is to say, he is looking towards Nuremberg from the west.

It is very remarkable to observe how he divides the picture into two halves: the fortified town to the right and the country to the left, with between them a view of the zigzagging street which leads us from the middle distance to the background. He paints the distant buildings in light, vaporous tones as they lie there in the noonday sun. The centre of the town is dominated in the background by the broad expanse of the citadel. At the extreme left we see the Church of the Cemetery of St. John, which lay outside the gates.

Dürer far, far surpasses everything which had in his day been achieved by way of prospects of towns, e.g. in Schedel's *World-Chronicle* at the woodcuts of which he had perhaps helped to work during his apprenticeship to Wolgemut, and which had appeared in 1493 from the press of his godfather Anton Koberger.

The picture type with the division into two parts and the central road leading to the rear may have been suggested to him by the woodcut serving as a frontispiece to Augustine's *Civitas Dei*, which Johannes Amerbach had published in Basle in 1490. This was the publisher for whom Dürer himself there made the Terence woodcuts in 1492/93. In the *Civitas Dei* there is a road running along the walls of Babylon, whose inhabitants are mocking those of the Holy City of Zion in the other half of the woodcut. A whole world, however, separates the modest artistic achievement of this wood-engraver from Dürer's gifted *pleinair* vision.

Fir-Tree

10

Water and body colours. 295 × 196 mm.
Produced about 1495/1497 after the return from Italy.
London, British Museum.

Even before the first Italian journey Dürer had made single studies of lime-trees, which stood on the bastions of the Burgberg not far from his father's house in Nuremberg (Winkler 63 and 64).

Now, home once more, and painting in watercolours the magnificent landscapes with the *Pond in the Woods* (Plate 12) and the *Mills on a River* (Plate 13) in which tree and wood play such a decisive part, he devotes this special study to a fir-tree.

Like the pine forest to the right of the pond (Plate 12) the fir-tree is not presented in sharply detailed close observation. The artist looks up at the top of the tree from a certain distance. The trunk is dealt with quite summarily. The tapering oval of the crown of a fir, the hanging branches, the swaying of the boughs with their turned-up ends and with only their young shoots set off clearly against the background—this is what Dürer wishes once for all to observe exactly and transfer to paper. And these young, light-green shoots tell us that he painted this watercolour in the month of May.

11 *House on an Island in a Pond*

Water and body colours. 213 × 222 mm. Below, Dürer's inscription 'Weier Haws'
and the monogram added by another hand.
Produced about 1495/1497 after the return from Italy.
London, British Museum.

The tower-shaped half-timbered building is supposed to have lain near Nuremberg on an island in the middle of a kind of pond formed by an obstruction in the Pegnitz. It is said, too, that the house served as a place of refuge for Nuremberg councillors in time of war.

The mood induced by the multitude of clear water-surfaces is a peaceful one; but it is menaced not merely by the yellowy red glare of the evening sky and its dark banks of clouds, but also by the violent curve of the boat, which alone can bear us over to the security of the house on the island.

Dürer used this landscape as a background in his famous engraving *Madonna with the Monkey* (Bartsch 42), taking over from the watercolour even the cloud formation and the spiralling broom bush.

12 *Pond in the Woods*

Water and body colours. 262 × 374 mm. Top middle Dürer's monogram
added by another hand. Produced about 1495/1497 after the return from Italy.
London, British Museum.

Daybreak on a small lake in the woods.

It was an unheard-of undertaking to paint such a fleeting mood in nature with these strong colours.

The blue clouds of night are still in the sky, whilst others are tinted in delicate yellow by the rising sun not yet in view. No breath of wind ruffles the water. No image is reflected by it; it merely brightens away towards the horizon under a lighter sky. The reeds and grasses, seen separated by his keen-sighted observation and put in with body colour, detach themselves individually. The red trunks of the pine-trees to the right are drawn together into a real wood.

At bottom right and top left the sheet remains so unfinished that it is not even covered with a light wash. The tops of the left group of trees are also missing, perhaps in order not to encroach upon the clouds, perhaps because the splendour of colour in such an hour of early light fades all too quickly, more quickly than even a rapid brush can seize it.

13 *Mills on a River*

Water and body colours. 251 × 367 mm. Top left Dürer's inscription 'Weydenmull'
and the monogram added by another hand.
Produced about 1495/1497 after the return from Italy.
Paris, Bibliothèque Nationale.

Even the two glorious watercolours *House on an Island in a Pond* (Plate 11) and *Pond in the Woods* (Plate 12), with their impressions of evening and morning are surpassed by the bold splendour of colour in these *Mills on a River*.

16

Dürer here paints the way in which, after spring thunder, the light breaks through again. It makes the clouds glow red and orange, colours the spring foliage of the magnificent willows emerald green and causes it to glisten damply.

The mills on the Pegnitz, which Dürer here portrays, lay to the west of Nuremberg near the Hallerwiesen. It is the same group of buildings as that which he depict d from the north in his well-known early watercolour as *Wire-drawing Mill* (Winkler 61). Here, however, he is again standing on the north bank of the river but looking from east to west.

What a development the artist has undergone in a few years from the still somewhat awkward beginnings to such bold mastery! Then he had chosen a high horizon and had given a sober topographical representation, without any characterization of the time of day. Now, however, he is master of space and perspective in quite a different way. From a low viewpoint he chooses the picture sector very ably; and with flat watercolours ventures to trap on the sheet the splendour of a rare and evanescent hour.

14   *Jousting Helmet in Three Views*

Brush drawing in water and body colours; the helmet top left first sketched in
with the pen. 422 × 268 mm. Bottom left Dürer's monogram in his own
hand. Above, a second monogram and the date 1514 added by another hand.
Produced about 1498.
Paris, Musée du Louvre.

The artist's cheerful scrupulosity in the study of an object is very clearly shown by this sheet. It shows the jousting helmet in profile and in the front and rear view. And then the watercolour has to characterize with the utmost exactitude the blue of the steel, the light reflections on the shining metal, the brass buttons, the brown cords and green straps.

The upper two studies were used by Dürer as models in the engraving *Coat of Arms with the Skull* (Bartsch 101, dated 1503) and *Coat of Arms with the Cock* (Bartsch 100). The colours and tone-values have there been transferred into the black and white of the graphic medium.

A helmet which largely corresponds to that in Dürer's sheet of studies is now in the Higgins Armoury, Worcester (Mass.). It forms part of a suit of armour made by the Nuremberg smith Valentin Siebenbürger, and the claim has been made (in Art News, Vol. 38, 1940, No. 28, p. 20) that it served as a model for Dürer. As Siebenbürger, however, was not born until 1510 and only became a master in 1531, none of his works can have been used by Dürer as a pattern.

The helmet at Worcester must either have been made on the basis of Dürer's drawing, or, and this is the more likely, both it and Dürer follow an older helmet. This, I conjecture, may have originated with Hans Grünwalt, one of Nuremberg's most important smiths, who was for example in 1496, just like Dürer, working for Frederick the Wise of Saxony, and who died in 1503. His workshop was taken over by his son-in-law, Wilhelm of Worms, the father-in-law and predecessor of Valentin Siebenbürger.

17

Brush drawing with watercolour. 317 × 172 mm.
Above, monogram in Dürer's own hand, and date 1500.
London, British Museum.

Dürer himself in an inscription indicated what he was here representing: *Eine Nörmergerin als man zw Kirchen gatt* (A Nuremberg Lady going to Church).

In the Albertina in Vienna there is a duplicate in which the contours are drawn with a pen. In quality and freshness it is inferior to the London sheet; in format and technique it forms part of a series of costume studies which consists of the following four sheets:

Nuremberg Lady Dressed for Church (Winkler 224)
Nuremberg Lady Dressed for a Dance (Winkler 225)
Nuremberg Lady Dressed for the Home (Winkler 226)
Nuremberg Girl Dressed for a Dance (Winkler 227)

The big, starched linen cap and the attractive pleated wrap were, as one may see from this series, only worn by the Nuremberg women to go to church. It is fascinating to speculate on the way in which Dürer used such costume studies in his graphic picture compositions.

This very *Nuremberg Lady Dressed for Church* appears in the woodcut *Betrothal of the Virgin* (Bartsch 82, about 1504) as the Virgin's companion, for the good reason that the scene is set in the temple. For Dürer and his contemporaries it was less important to present Biblical figures in historically correct than in realistically lifelike costume. From these contemporary costumes the one chosen would be that most suitable to the occasion, and thus, for a visit to the temple, the church dress.

As the *Nuremberg Girl Dressed for a Dance* appears in the engraving *Coat of Arms with a Skull* (Bartsch 101, dated 1503) the costume becomes important for the symbolical interpretation of the latter. The girl, we must suppose, has taken her place for the dance, the dance of death, which the supporter, a savage, seems to be asking her for.

16   *Young Hare*

Water and body colours. 251 × 226 mm.
Below, monogram in Dürer's own hand and date 1502.
Vienna, Albertina.

Dürer's precise brush here celebrates its greatest triumph. For there is scarcely any water-colour, by any other artist, which enjoys such world-wide fame and which so fascinates all hearts.

It is absorbing to compare the very different 'viewpoint' which Dürer chose for this sheet and for the *Great Piece of Turf* (Plate 17). Standing or sitting Dürer, and we with him, looks down on the 'Young Hare.' As when danger threatens in the open fields the hare alertly pricks up its great ears; warm and soft as it is painted, and attractive as it is of itself, it moreover seems to us to need protection.

It had clearly been possible to catch the model, a young wild hare, alive, and this must have given Dürer the opportunity to 'portray' it here. For it is a very difficult undertaking to keep these shy creatures in perpetual captivity, and the begetting and rearing of young under such conditions is even more rare. At any rate the hare was kept in a room when Dürer painted it, perhaps in his studio. This is indicated by the cross-bar of the window, which is reflected in the creature's eye and the smooth surfaces on which it casts its shadow.

17   *The Great Piece of Turf*

Water and body colours. 410 × 315 mm.
Bottom right, scarcely visible, dated 1503.
Vienna, Albertina.

What boldness on the part of the young Dürer to take it into his head to paint a perfectly ordinary piece of meadowland. And then not, for instance, the uniform green carpet of the earth as seen from above!

Dürer must have lain on the ground to sketch the piece of turf from a close frontal view and in natural size. That is why it gives the effect of looking into the undergrowth of a primeval forest. The undergrowth is however kept quite clear and it is possible to recognize plainly in it yarrow and plantain, dandelion, pimpernel and different kinds of grasses.

18   *Madonna with a Multitude of Animals*

Pen and watercolour. 321 × 243 mm. Produced about 1503.
Vienna, Albertina.

This is the most important composition amongst Dürer's pictorial watercolours and is one of his most attractive works in general.

How easily and with what little effort the pen has here put down the multiplicity and the brush coloured dreamlike all that the master has invented. Mary is sitting with the Christchild, who holds in both hands a strawberry sprig, on a grassy seat with mallow and columbine, irises and peonies in bloom all around. In peaceable, paradisal proximity a multitude of animals surrounds her: eagle-owl, barn-owl and crab (cf. Plate 2), fox and hound (cf. Plate 1), stag-beetle, dragon fly, snail, woodpecker and all kinds of other birds. At Mary's head a great star is shining, and an angel announces the glad tidings to the shepherds in the fields at the edge of the woods.

The Berlin Kupferstichkabinett possesses a rough drawing for the whole (Winkler 295), and the Louvre a watercolour variant dated 1503 (Winkler 297).

Many details, as for example the parrot and the stork in the background, remind us of previous sheets of studies (Winkler 244 and 240). Other figures are to be met with in Dürer's prints. This does not mean that he repeats himself. The very point of his drawing so tirelessly was that he could incorporate as securely mastered detail in his later compositions what he had studied individually.

Portrait of an Architect,
probably of Master Hieronymus (Girolamo Tedescho)

Black brush drawing, heightened with white, on blue Venetian paper. 386 × 263 mm.
Bottom left, monogram in Dürer's own hand and date 1506.
Formerly Berlin, Staatliches Kupferstichkabinett.

From the letters which Dürer wrote from Venice to Pirkheimer in Nuremberg we know that, between January and the beginning of September 1506, he painted there as a commission for 'the Germans' a large altar panel. It is the *Feast of the Rose Garlands* (Prague, National Gallery), which was originally set up in the burial chapel of the German colony on the high altar of S. Bartolomeo on the Rialto.

According to Sansovino in his *Venezia Città nobilissima* (1581) this Madonna picture was donated by one of the Fuggers. It is, however, quite possible that it was the German merchants of the Fondaco dei Tedeschi who commissioned the altar panel jointly.

Despite much damage and restoration, the work remains Dürer's sublimest painting. Mary, the Christchild and St. Dominic, the founder of the Cult of the Rosary, are crowning Pope Julius II, the Emperor Maximilian and other representatives spiritual and temporal with garlands of red and white roses. Most of the kneeling figures will be those very German merchants who were then resident in Venice. In the middle distance stands Dürer himself, with a paper in his hand and on it his inscription and the year 1506.

An architect, characterized by the ruler, is kneeling in the second row on the right-hand edge of the picture. Our drawing is a study for this man. An old tradition makes him Girolamo Tedescho, the German master Hieronymus (of Augsburg?), from whose designs was rebuilt in those years (1505–1508), near the Rialto, the House of the German Merchants in Venice, the Fondaco dei Tedeschi.

Of the studies for the *Feast of the Rose Garlands* which have survived this sheet is one of the most perfect; it is a portrait full of life of an energetic man whose eyes are looking prophetically into the distance, and whose mouth betrays idealism and artistic inventiveness.

I conjecture that one of the motives for Dürer's journey to Venice in the autumn of 1505 was that he hoped to be given a part in the provision of paintings to decorate the Fondaco, which Master Girolamo had designed in the middle of the same year. This is all the more to be supposed as there are among the drawings of the Venetian period a few sheets that, in my opinion, must be regarded as drafts for monumental paintings and which, judging by their themes, would have been suitable for frescoes in the Fondaco, which was at the same time the seat of the Court of the Visdomini of the Fondaco: e.g. *The Judgement of Solomon* (Winkler 376); *The Justice of Trajan* (Winkler 446); for a façade painting e.g. the *Allegorical Figure of a Woman with a Mirror* (Winkler 460).

The Venetian government, however, obviously wanted to employ only native artists for the completion of their important new building on the Grand Canal. It appears that the German master Hieronymus was sent to work on fortifications in Cattaro, whilst the direction of the building was entrusted to the Venetian architect Antonio Abbondi and the general superintendence to Giorgio Spavento. The Senate resolved that the façades should not be adorned with costly marblework and reliefs but merely with frescoes, and had these executed by Giorgione from Castelfranco, as whose assistant the young Titian first emerges with his work on the façades of the flanks (1508).

How much more obvious it was, then, that the German merchants should commission from Dürer the picture for the high altar in their church – a matter in which they could act quite independently of any interference by the Senate. Dürer's disappointed hopes in the Fondaco affair would also be in line with the complaints in his letters about jealousy, intrigues and criticism on the part of his Venetian colleagues, who "blame my thing... and say it is not ancient in style and thus is not good," as well as with his exultation on completion of the *Feast of the Rose Garlands*: "...And I have silenced all the painters who said I was good as an engraver but did not know how to handle the colours in painting. Now they all say that they have never seen more beautiful colours... and I herewith wish it to be understood that there is no better picture of the Virgin in the country" (to Pirkheimer, 8 and 23 September 1506).

It also agrees very well with such incidents and struggles over prestige that the Doge and the Patriarch of Venice should finally have viewed Dürer's panel, as he proudly informs Pirkheimer (8 September 1506).

20   *Angel*

Brush drawing in Indian ink, heightened with white, on blue Venetian paper.
270 × 208 mm. Left, monogram in Dürer's own hand and date 1506.
Vienna, Albertina.

This head, with the beauty and perfection of which very little in the whole of Dürer's great *oeuvre* can compare, served the artist as a preliminary study for the angel who is playing the lute at the Virgin's feet in the *Feast of the Rose Garlands*.

The sheet is, like the portrait drawing of the *Architect* (Plate 19) in the same picture, still preserved in a very fresh state both as regards the linework of the brush strokes and also the blue of the paper. Originally the head was on one sheet with that of the *Twelve-Year-Old Jesus* (Winkler 404), a study for the picture in the Thyssen Collection at Lugano which Dürer also painted in Venice in 1506. The two drawings were therefore separated later. Both are to be considered not as studies from nature but as ideal sketches of sacred figures.

The verve and grace of the head of Dürer's angel, and indeed the whole appearance of the lute-player in the painting, are inspired by the angels in Giovanni Bellini's Madonna pictures (Altar from S. Giobbe, Venice, Accademia, about 1490—Murano, S. Pietro Martire, 1488,—Venice, S. Zaccaria, 1505).

Among the many good painters whom Dürer came across in Venice, he most esteemed 'Sambelling' (as he calls Giambellin): "He is very old and still the best in painting" he wrote to Pirkheimer (7 February 1506).

21   *Nude Woman seen from the Back*

Brush drawing in Indian ink, heightened with white, on blue Venetian paper.
283 × 224 mm. Below, monogram in Dürer's own hand, above, the date 1506.
Formerly Berlin, Staatliches Kupferstichkabinett.

Dürer's noblest nude drawing as regards the graphic execution in dark and light cross-hatchings, the proportioning and the harmony of the outline.

Alongside the figure the ground has been washed with Indian ink so that the figure should detach itself the more plastically from suggested depth in space. In her outstretched hand the woman is holding a cap, a device which has the effect of allowing the left contour of the body to run in a free line without intersection from the crown of the head to the sole of the foot.

It is no accident that the drawing was produced in Venice. The peculiar position of the feet, the way the head is held and the view from the back are all closely connected with Giorgione's *Prudenza*, formerly in the entrance hall of the Palazzo Grimani near San Marcuola. The nobility of this model did not fail to have its effect on Dürer.

The use of streaks of reflected light which illuminate the dark areas of shadow (most evident here along the right contour of the body) may also perhaps be an indebtedness to that fresco of Giorgione's which has perished, and which is only known to us by a copy existing in England (Mirfield Collection). But it would not have been impossible for Dürer to have made this advance for himself through his own studies and stimulated by Leonardo's doctrine (Treatise on Painting, paras. 158–162). We know, indeed, that Dürer was made familiar with some of the ideas of Leonardo and Piero della Francesca, when he rode specially from Venice to Bologna "for the sake of art in secret perspective, which someone wishes to teach me" (to Pirkheimer, 13 October 1506).

The Metropolitan Museum in New York possesses a stone plaque, with Dürer's monogram and dated 1509, which a sculptor in his entourage produced on the basis of this sheet and related nude drawings.

22   *Project Drawing for the All Saints Picture*

Pen drawing with watercolour. 391 × 263 mm.
Below, middle, marked: 'Anno dom. 1508' and monogram.
Chantilly, Musée Condé.

Our drawing was completed by Dürer in 1508 for Matthias Landauer as the first full sketch for a work with which the latter had commissioned him, a retable for the altar of the All Saints Chapel of the Zwölfbrüderhaus, a home for twelve aged Nuremberg citizens, founded by the rich Landauer and Erasmus Schildkrot.

The painting, which was not completed until 1511, is now in Vienna (Kunsthistorisches Museum), the frame in Nuremberg (Germanisches Nationalmuseum). In comparison with the sketch both have undergone quite important changes, of which one only may be mentioned, namely that the picture contains portraits of the donor Matthias Landauer and his son-in-law Wilhelm Haller, and also of Dürer himself, holding a tablet with his signature.

Apart from this project drawing for the *All Saints Picture* only one similar full sketch for a picture survives, that for the pictures of the Emperors in the Nuremberg Heiltumskammer (Winkler 503). Both show the whole of the picture, including the frame, and are executed in the same way technically; that is to say, they are drawn with the pen and touched up 'in half colours,' as Dürer himself called the light application of a watercolour wash.

The square area, which is coloured in our sketch, is what Dürer planned to paint. All the rest, that is the frame with the columns, ornamentation and figurative work was to be executed in wood by a wood-carver.

The title of the All Saints Chapel and Altar already indicates the theme of the picture: the communion of all saints, the very old idea of the *Civitas Dei*. In it the Church Triumphant, the triumphant Communion of Saints in Heaven is ranged around the triune Godhead. God the Father holds the crucified Son to his bosom. Above him hovers the Holy Ghost in the form of a dove. Angels spread out the mantle of the Father. On his right the Virgin kneels, behind her St. Catherine and other holy virgins; on his left John the Baptist at the head of male saints. Further below Pope, cardinal, bishop and monks as representatives of the hierarchy in the New Covenant, and over against them King David, Moses and patriarchs of the Old Covenant. All hover over the earth, on which the Church Militant, the community still engaged in the struggle of earthly life, is indicated merely by a church building.

Above, in a half-circular-shaped area the wood-carver was to depict the Last Judgement with Christ as the Judge of the World throned on the rainbow, and Mary and John as interceders for the 'Community of Sorrows' in the underworld. This community is represented on the frieze of the frame by those risen from the dead, who forthwith divide themselves into two groups: into the Blessed, who follow Peter to the left into the light of Heaven, and the Damned, who are dragged by devils to the right into the jaws of Hell.

If the intertwined ornamentation in the panelling of the frame is late Gothic in character, yet the whole construction of the frame represents one of the earliest Renaissance works in Germany. No other sheet in all Dürer's drawings speaks to us in such pure Italian forms, forms which he had seen in Venice and Padua, Verona and Bologna and which he here manipulates surely and independently.

23   *Standing Apostle*

Black brush drawing, heightened with white, on green-grounded paper. 400 × 235 mm.
Above, monogram in Dürer's own hand and date 1508.
Formerly Berlin, Staatliches Kupferstichkabinett.

In 1508, as a commission for the Frankfurt town councillor Jakob Heller, Dürer painted for the Dominican church there a folding altar, the middle panel of which was destroyed by fire in the eighteenth century. Dürer's letters to his patron in the years from 1507 to 1509 and his studies are the most important documents for this picture, except for a copy made by Jobst Harrich in 1614.

The centre panel showed at the top the Coronation of the Virgin in Heaven by the Father and the Son, and below on earth the twelve apostles, who, mourning and dismayed, surround the empty grave of the Mother of God and look up to her triumph in Heaven.

Our drawing served as a study for the apostle, Paul or James the Elder, standing in the foreground. In a further sheet (Winkler 448) Dürer studied in detail the head, which is only summarily indicated here because the purpose was to fix the total figure and particularly the draperies with their magnificent play of light and dark folds.

The way in which Dürer gives the figure character and force by the weight of the garment is wholly masterly. By having the apostle turn his back on the world he gives perfect expression to his willing surrender to a supernatural occurrence.

23

Black brush drawing, heightened with white, on blue-grounded paper.
290 × 197 mm. Produced in 1508.
Vienna, Albertina.

The study served as a model for the hands of that apostle who, in the *Heller Altar*, was kneeling at the right hand edge of the picture and gazing up reverently at the crowned Queen of Heaven. It was originally on the same sheet as the drawing of the head of the same apostle (Winkler 452), which has the monogram and the date 1508, but they were later separated.

In contrast to the other sixteen drawings for the Frankfurt altar these two are not green but blue-grounded. It is therefore assumed that Dürer here started his preliminary work for the Heller Altar by first so preparing his white paper that it should look like the natural blue Venetian paper, of which he had evidently run out.

Our study is one of the most famous of Dürer's works. The expressive power of these hands joined in prayer has always been admired and praised. Every detail is modelled with the finest brush, so that the effect approaches that of a pen drawing.

25   *Kalchreuth*

Water and body colours. 216 × 314 mm. Above, middle, Dürer's superscription
'Kalkrewt.' The monogram added by another hand.
Probably produced about 1511.
Formerly Bremen, Kunsthalle.

Kalchreuth lies about three leagues north-east of Nuremberg. The view of the village given by Dürer is from a little castle on a height, then belonging to the Nuremberg patrician family Haller. In contrast to the fortified towns, which are sharply detached from the landscape, the village is here allowed by Dürer really to grow into nature, a process in which the trees and the surface of the pond in the middle distance play a particularly important role.

In comparison with the other landscapes and their lack of people the motif of the two peasants sitting under the two magnificent, leafy trees is very unusual.

This landscape is truly masterly and is seen as one whole. In a few colours Dürer has painted everything with a broad sweep and with a uniform degree of emphasis, without presenting any one object in more detail than another. The September afternoon sun lies over the land and gives it a touch of ripeness and of harvest.

In that district hops are grown and are stored under the high hip-roofs. That is why, in late summer, the thatched roofs are opened for ventilation, as Dürer shows in the left foreground.

A second sheet, from a somewhat lower viewpoint, shows only the chain of the Frankish Jura, which forms the background of this sheet (Winkler 117). It has been justly pointed out (Tietze) that there is a connexion between the Jura watercolour and the landscape in the *All Saints Picture* of 1511, which has traits in it quite different from those of the full sketch of 1508 (Plate 22). I take it therefore, on stylistic grounds too, that Dürer painted both the Kalchreuth watercolours about the same year, 1511. This is all the more likely as the *All*

Saints Picture contains a portrait of Wilhelm Haller and his wife, a proof that Dürer was at this time in personal contact with the Hallers. Kalchreuth was formerly in the possession of Wolf Haller (d. 1508), who had married in 1491 Ursula, daughter of the publisher Anton Koberger who was Dürer's godfather. After he had abandoned her and had put himself and his estates in Kalchreuth and elsewhere under the feudal protection of the Margrave of Brandenburg he quarrelled with Koberger and the Nuremberg Council, which called him "its disobedient and faithless citizen" (June 1506).

26   *Little Chandelier Woman*

Brush and pen drawing with watercolour. 153 × 195 mm.
Top middle, date 1513 in Dürer's own hand.
Vienna, Kunsthistorisches Museum.

On the coat of arms intersected by the woman's left arm we may recognize a small birch tree: the bearings of the Councillor and humanist Willibald Pirkheimer.

Airy lightness and grace, such as one finds only rarely in Dürer, mark this sketch for a chandelier, which he jotted down for his old friend.

The antlers which spread like a pair of wings around the garlanded head of the beautiful siren are, exceptionally, not here intended to hold the candles. That is the function of the shoots of plants which the woman is holding in her hands.

27   *Arion*

Preliminary drawing with a brush; watercolour wash; finally contours gone over with a pen.
142 × 234 mm. Produced about 1514.
Vienna, Kunsthistorisches Museum.

The drawing comes from the *Kunstbuch Albrethen dürers aus Nürnberg*, a volume pieced together of Dürer's graphic works and drawings, which originates from the collection of the Archduke Ferdinand of Tirol in Schloss Ambras. To the same volume belong also the technically and stylistically related mythological representations of a *Water Nymph, Hermes, Venus and Amor* (Winkler 663–665). Since the last-named sheet is dated 1514, the present one is rightly enough assigned to the same period.

The Latin verse which Dürer has written on the upper edge explains the theme of the picture: PISCE SUPER CURVO VECTUS CANTABAT ARION—Borne along through the waves by a fish Arion sang. Arion was a poet from Methymna on Lesbos, living in the 7th century B.C. According to the legend passed on already by Herodotus (about 500 B.C.) and later by many Greek and Roman writers, he was threatened on the high seas by seamen who wished to rob him. Striking one more chord on his lyre he sprang into the sea, and was rescued by a dolphin which carried him away through the waves. The synthesis of expressive power, verve and grace make this one of Dürer's most beautiful mythological representations, in which he approaches the spirit of antiquity.

It is known that for Arion and Hermes he followed a sketch by the Nuremberg doctor Hartmann Schedel (1440–1514.—Munich, Staatsbibliothek, Cod. lat. 716). Schedel, who studied in Padua, entered in his codex a transcript of the diary of a journey in Greece by Cyriacus of Ancona (1391–1452) and copied its drawings. Between depictions of Athenian sculptures we find Arion on a dolphin, accompanied by the same verse as that which Dürer wrote on his sheet. It will be a relief in Athens which Cyriacus drew, and on which, in the last analysis, Dürer's work is based. Such reliefs may already have originally adorned Pericles's Odeon, all the more so as it was later rebuilt in 52 B.C. by two Roman architects according to the old plan. One may also suppose that such relief decoration existed on the concert hall and theatre, which Herodes Atticus built there in 161–165 A.D.

Dürer's four mythological sheets of 1514 may have been intended as free, individual watercolours, or perhaps as drafts of illustrations for a projected book by Hartmann Schedel, who had indeed published his famous *World-Chronicle* in 1493 in the printing-office of Dürer's godfather Anton Koberger. In any case it is striking that the sheets were produced in the year of Schedel's death. In the same year 1514 the famous *Commentarii* of Cyriacus of Ancona in the possession of the Sforzas at Pesaro were destroyed by fire; Dürer's intimate friend Pirkheimer must have known them at least in transcript, and perhaps, as a friend of the Sforzas, even in the original.

It is by no means impossible that the group of mythological sheets to which Arion on the Dolphin belongs must be connected with Pirkheimer.

Indeed I regard it as highly probable and that for the following reasons. Dürer's Hermes drawing is based, as is known, on a passage in Lucian. He may also have found the Arion legend in Lucian, in his *Dialogi marini* (Panofsky). That the legend's contents were familiar to Dürer is shown not only by his divergences from the sketch in Schedel-Cyriacus but also by his correction of the error 'Orion' in Schedel's annotation. He will have got to know Lucian's writings through Pirkheimer, who was a connoisseur of Lucian and was his translator.

After the death of Dürer and Pirkheimer the Hermes drawing served as the model for the woodcut frontispiece to Apianus' and Amantius' *Inscriptiones sacrosanctae vetustatis* (Ingolstadt 1534). The two authors made use, as they say in their book, of epigraphic notes and drawings by Pirkheimer. His literary remains were therefore accessible to them. It is thus very probable that Dürer's Hermes sheet was among them. In addition there is the fact that the *Little Chandelier Woman* (Plate 26), obviously made for Pirkheimer and including his coat of arms, is associated in the same collection at Vienna with the four mythological sheets of 1514; all five come from the Ambras art book. Archduke Ferdinand may very well have obtained them jointly from the same source.

28   *Sketch for Courtly Garb*

Pen and watercolour. 282 × 210 mm. Produced about 1515/1517.
Vienna, Albertina.

On the verso of the sheet the same man is to be found in a side view, and in another drawing in the Albertina he completely turns his back to us. The artist has thus carefully drawn his model from all sides, so that there should be no mistake as to how the robe would look all around.

The violet garment displays a light-green lining with which the delicate pink border facings are in the most beautiful harmony. The yellow edging was certainly to be executed in gold. The speed with which Dürer worked is shown by the fact that the pen drawing was not yet quite dry when he dashed on the watercolours, making the ink run in some places.

The sheet belongs, to all appearances, with that group of works which Dürer produced for Maximilian I in 1512–1519. The court costume which Dürer here designs lets us catch a glimpse of the magnificence and colourfulness which the Emperor liked to see in his retinue. That Dürer was called in to devise such things will not surprise us, for Leonardo as court painter for the Duke of Milan had also to sketch costumes, designs for material and decorations for festivals.

29   *Study for the Head in a Madonna Picture*

Size colour on fine canvas. 255 × 215 mm. Produced about 1520.
Paris, Bibliothèque Nationale.

The Dürer literature usually ranges this watercolour study with the paintings, probably because it is painted on canvas.

The work is, in places, in bad condition, but the damage is trifling when one considers that the artist applied the colours directly to the unprepared canvas. The contour of the left cheek, which originally projected further, was corrected by Dürer himself.

Both as regards the dating and the interpretation of this study there have been pretty contradictory proposals made. Pierre du Colombier was the first to assign it to the period of the Journey to the Netherlands about 1520, though it was then conjecturally dated 1497. He also justly refuted the prevailing idea that it was the artist's wife, Agnes Dürer, who was here depicted.

This sublime head has indeed nothing in common with the prosaic ill-humour of Agnes Dürer.

There is a good deal of evidence for the view that this study (certainly an ideal head, and probably a 'constructed' one, that is to say, a head built up according to a certain system of proportions) represents an endeavour to create a new Madonna type. It seems to me that here Dürer had at the back of his mind an early Dutch Madonna painting with a broad, flat type of face and low forehead, like, for instance, the Master of Flémalle's Salting Madonna (London, National Gallery).

It is a noteworthy fact that the painter, as in other heads of the period of the Journey to the Netherlands, not only chooses the plain frontal view and lays out the background dark, but also gives it no emotionally accentuated inclination to either side. The strictly erect nature of the 'carriage' is an important feature of some of Dürer's figures from the period of his maturity from the Journey to the Netherlands until his death (1520–1528).

The two heads of boys on the same kind of canvas in the same collection are, similarly, not to be regarded as studies from nature but as the putting to canvas of ideas for pictures. The turn of the head and the glance attest this. They could be studies for the heads of the Infants Christ and John in the same projected Madonna picture.

27

Brush drawing in Indian ink, heightened with white, on greyish-violet-grounded paper.
420 × 282 mm. Top left, monogram and date 1521 in Dürer's own hand.
Vienna, Albertina.

On the upper edge of the sheet Dürer noted: "The man, at Antwerp, was 93 and still healthy and in possession of his faculties." We have before us, therefore, the drawing of an old man of 93, whom Dürer portrayed in Antwerp during his Journey to the Netherlands. That will have been at the beginning of January 1521, when he wrote in his journal: "Item, gave three stuivers to the man I portrayed." According to this the old man had not himself commissioned a portrait, but had been asked by the painter to sit as his model.

The magnificent sheet served as a preliminary study to the painting *St. Jerome* (Lisbon, National Museum), as did a few further drawings, among them the *Reading-Desk* (Plate 31).

This picture is mentioned by Dürer in his journal on 16 March 1521: "I have painstakingly done a St. Jerome in oils and have presented it to Rodrigo of Portugal." The painter therefore gave it as a present to Rodrigo Fernandez d'Almada, the Portuguese Agent in Antwerp, to whom he was indebted for various valuable gifts.

In the same technique on greyish-violet-grounded paper, just as in the studies for the St. Jerome picture, Dürer drew at the beginning of April 1521 a brilliant portrait of Rodrigo d'Almada himself (Winkler 813), about which he notes in his journal: "And I have portrayed Ruderigo on a large sheet of paper by a brush drawing in black and white."

The splendid format of about 16 inches height and the clean brushwork in black Indian ink and white were noteworthy even for Dürer—how much the more so for us! "The great brush drawing in the Albertina is wholly overwhelming in its effect," writes Wölfflin about this study: "In this sheet there is so much greatness and so much simplicity, so much devotion to the minute products of nature at work and so much power in the comprehensive vision, that one may well speak of the beginning of a new style in Dürer."

31 *Reading-Desk with Books*

Brush drawing in Indian ink, heightened with white, on greyish-violet-grounded paper.
198 × 280 mm. Below, monogram in Dürer's own hand and date 1521.
Vienna, Albertina.

How attractive and impressive this drawing is in the simplicity of its motif and in its arrangement on the paper! It is one of the earliest still-life studies in German art. The still life was then painted in oils only indeed as a detail in a figure picture. The reading-desk stands, near the inkwell and the skull, on the table in front of *St. Jerome* (Lisbon, National Museum) who rests his head musingly on his right hand and points to the skull with his left.

In the painting the left edge of the picture cuts off about a third of the reading-desk, and thus the thin oval box drops out and Dürer confines himself to the grouping of the desk and the books.

The Annunciation

Pen with watercolour. 288 × 211 mm.
Top right, monogram and date 1526 in Dürer's own hand.
Chantilly, Musée Condé.

In the vaulted room, magnificently fitted out with circular window and oil-lamp, plate rack, draped walls and cushioned bench, the Madonna has been seated on a raised throne under a canopy. Overpowered by the appearance of the angel she drops to her knees between the throne and the reading-desk. The angel holds in his left hand a heavily sealed document as a visible sign that he is making a solemn proclamation as God's herald. On a beam of light from Heaven the dove of the Holy Ghost, the power of the Most High descends and throws its shadow over the Virgin.

It is a late work of Dürer's, novel and great in its conception, the penmanship perfect in its freedom and certainty, the 'half colours' in which it is washed delicate and indeed fresh.

LITERARY REFERENCES

As there are a great many careful and comprehensive Dürer bibliographies we merely indicate the four publications most important in our connexion.

FRIEDRICH LIPPMANN: *Zeichnungen von Albrecht Dürer*. 7 Vols. (Vols. 6 and 7 ed. by Friedrich Winkler). Berlin 1883–1929.

HANS TIETZE and ERIKA TIETZE-CONRAT: *Kritisches Verzeichnis der Werke Albrecht Dürers*. Vol. I: Augsburg 1928; Vol. II, 1 and 2: Basel 1937 and 1938.

FRIEDRICH WINKLER: *Die Zeichnungen Albrecht Dürers*. 4 Vols. Berlin 1936–1939.

ERWIN PANOFSKY: *Albrecht Dürer*. 2 Vols. Princeton, N.J. 1945.

The Dürer engravings referred to in this work are always designated as 'Bartsch' followed by the number under which they are to be found in

ADAM BARTSCH, *Le Peintre-Graveur*. Vol. 7. Vienne 1808.

PLATES

I

Young Couple on Horseback

Probably 1496. Pen and water-colour. 215 x 165 mm.

Formerly Berlin, Staatliches Kupferstichkabinett.

2

Sea Crab

Probably 1495. Water-colours and white body colour. 263 × 355 mm.

Vierhouten, D. G. van Beuningen Collection.

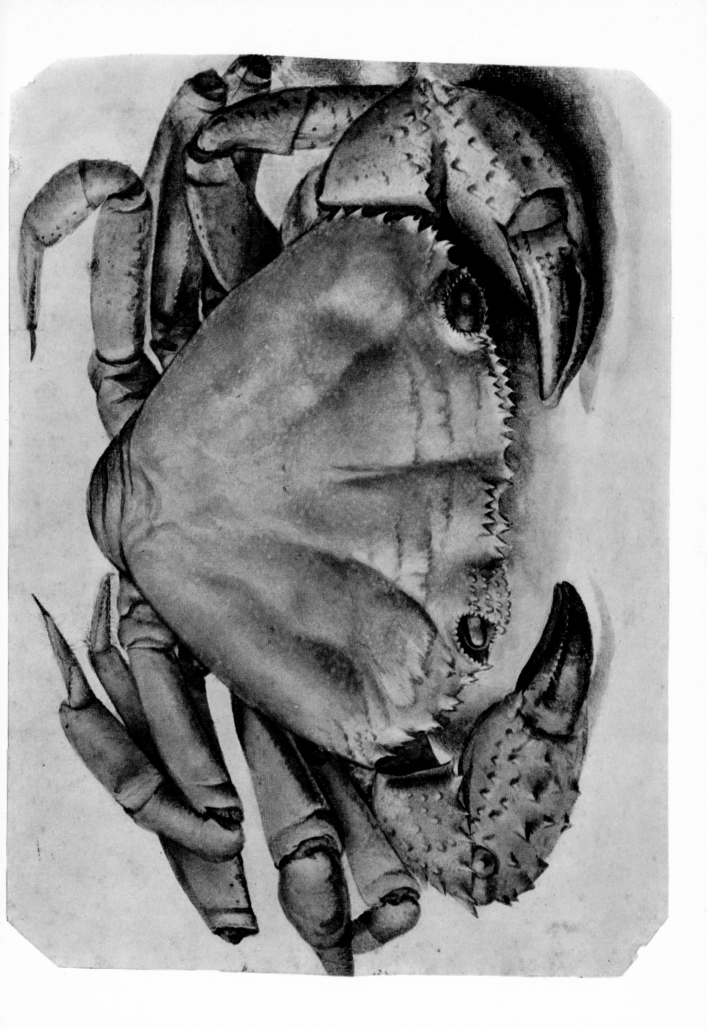

3

Arco

1495. Water and body colour. 221 x 221 mm.

Paris, Musée du Louvre.

4

The Castle of Trento

1495. Water-colour. 198 x 257 mm.

London, British Museum.

5

Trento seen from the North

1495. Water and body colours. 238 x 356 mm.

Formerly Bremen, Kunsthalle.

6

South-Tyrolean Mountain Scene

Probably 1495. Water and body colours. 210 × 312 mm.

Oxford, Ashmolean Museum.

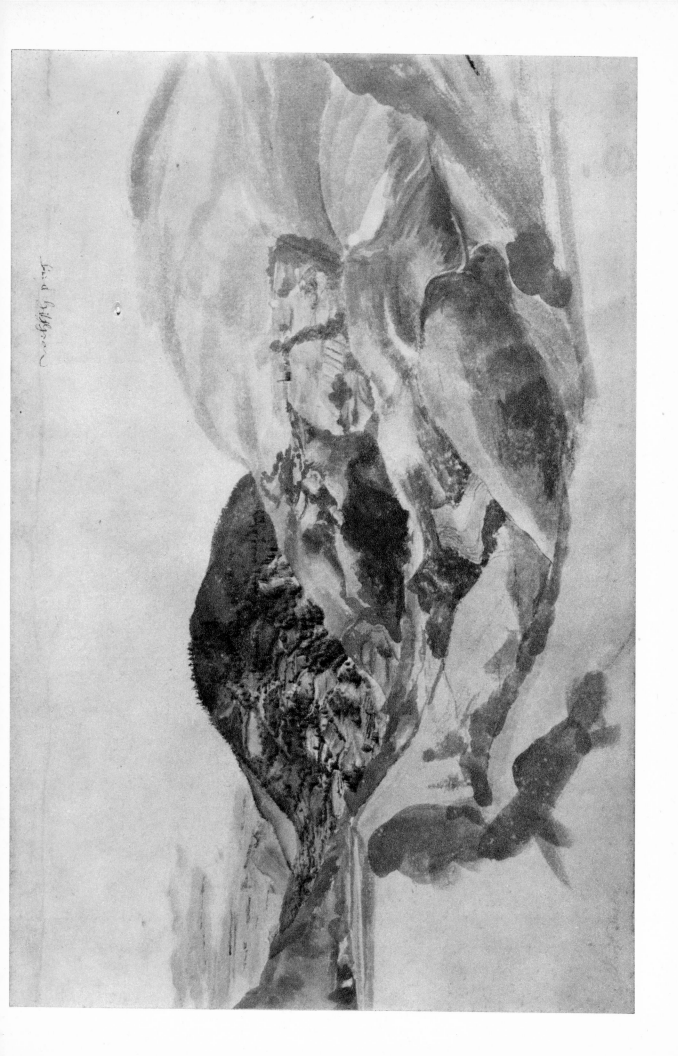

7

Innsbruck seen from the North

Probably 1495. Water-colour. 127 x 187 mm.

Vienna, Albertina.

8

Quarry

About 1495. Water-colour. 232 x 197 mm.

Milan, Biblioteca Ambrosiana.

9

Nuremberg seen from the West

About 1495/1497. Water and body colours. 163 × 344 mm.

Formerly Bremen, Kunsthalle.

Salzburg

Fir-Tree

About 1495/1497. Water and body colours. 295 x 196 mm.

London, British Museum.

II

House on an Island in a Pond

About 1495/1497. Water and body colours. 213 x 222 mm.

London, British Museum.

weier Haus

12

Pond in the Woods

About 1495/1497. Water and body colours. 262 x 374 mm.

London, British Museum.

Mills on a River

About 1495/1497. Water and body colours. 251 x 367 mm.

Paris, Bibliothèque Nationale.

14

Jousting Helmet in Three Views

About 1498. Brush drawing in water and body colours. 422 x 268 mm.

Paris, Musée du Louvre.

15

Nuremberg Lady Dressed for Church

1500. Brush drawing with water-colour. 317 × 172 mm.

London, British Museum.

16

Young Hare

1502. Water and body colours. 251 x 226 mm.

Vienna, Albertina.

17

The Great Piece of Turf

1503. Water and body colours. 410 × 315 mm.

Vienna, Albertina.

18

Madonna with a Multitude of Animals

About 1503. Pen and water-colour. 321 x 243 mm.

Vienna, Albertina.

19

Portrait of an Architect

probably of Master Hieronymus (Girolamo Tedescho)

1506. Brush drawing. 386 x 263 mm.

Formerly Berlin, Staatliches Kupferstichkabinett.

20

Angel

1506. Brush drawing. 270 x 208 mm.

Vienna, Albertina.

21

Nude Woman seen from the Back

1506. Brush drawing. 283 x 224 mm.

Formerly Berlin, Staatliches Kupferstichkabinett.

22

Project Drawing for the All Saints' Picture

1508. Pen drawing with water-colour. 391 x 263 mm.

Chantilly, Musée Condé.

23

Standing Apostle

1508. Brush drawing. 400 x 235 mm.

Formerly Berlin, Staatliches Kupferstichkabinett.

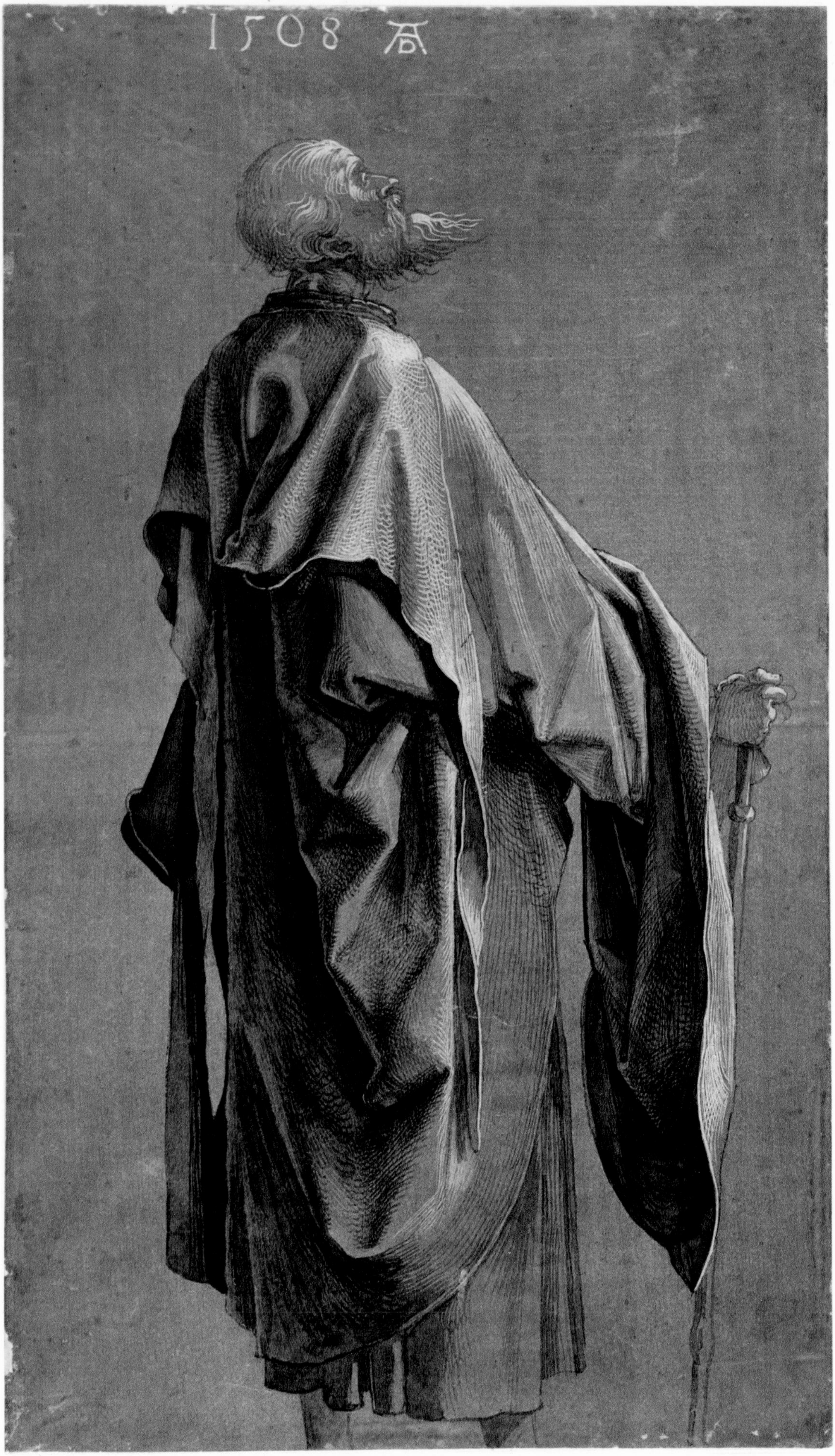
1508 AD

24

Hands Joined in Prayer

1508. Brush drawing. 290 x 197 mm.

Vienna, Albertina.

25

Kalchreuth

Probably about 1511. Water and body colours. 216 x 314 mm.

Formerly Bremen, Kunsthalle.

Kalk near. D

26

Little Chandelier· Woman

1513. Brush and pen drawing with water-colour. 153 x 195 mm.

Vienna, Kunsthistorisches Museum.

27

Arion

About 1514. Brush drawing and water-colour; contours gone over with a pen. 142 x 234 mm.

Vienna, Kunsthistorisches Museum.

PISCE SVPER CVRVO VECTVS CANTABAT ARION

28

Sketch for Courtly Garb

About 1515/1517. Pen with water-colour. 282 x 210 mm.

Vienna, Albertina.

29

Study for the Head in a Madonna Picture

About 1520. Size-colour on fine canvas. 255 × 215 mm.

Paris, Bibliothèque Nationale.

30

Portrait of an Old Man

1521. Brush drawing. 420 × 282 mm.

Vienna, Albertina.

31

Reading-Desk with Books

1521. Brush drawing. 198 × 280 mm.

Vienna, Albertina.

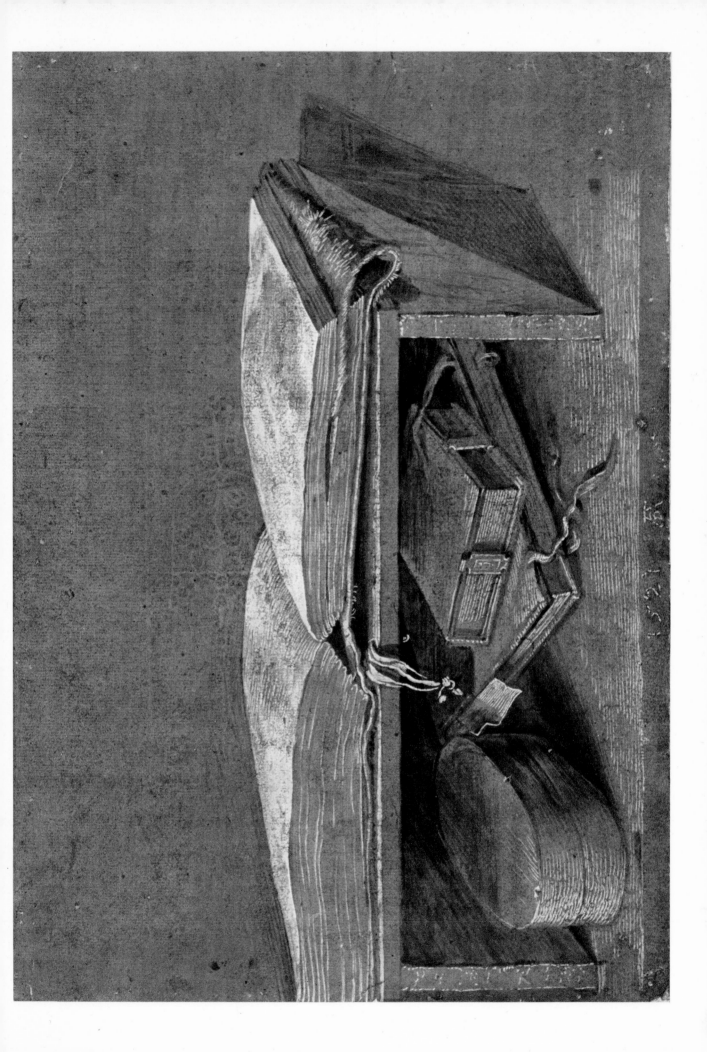

32

The Annunciation

1526. Pen with water-colour. 288 x 211 mm.

Chantilly, Musée Condé.

COLOUR PHOTOGRAPHS

Amsterdam, Foto-ateliers M. C. Meyboom: 2. — Frankfurt on Main/Höchst, Farbfoto-Studio Hermann Harz: 1, 21, 23. — Knebworth, Hertfordshire, Sir Geoffrey Cory-Wright: 4, 6, 10, 11, 12, 15. — Milan, Claudio Emmer: 8. — Paris, Louis Laniepce: 3, 13, 14, 22, 32. — Paris, André Thévenet: 29. — Vienna, C. Angerer & Göschl: 20, 26, 27, 28, 31.

Plates 5, 9, 19, and 25 are reproduced from Marées Facsimile prints of R. Piper & Co., Publishers, Munich; plates 7, 16, 17, 18, 24, and 30 from Albertina Facsimiles of Anton Schroll & Co., Publishers, Vienna.